Be A Food Allergy Helper!

by Lisa Woodruff, RDN
Illustrated by Olive Phan

Dedicated to E and A:

You are the best Food Allergy Helpers. I am so proud of you.

And to R:

You inspired me to become a food allergy advocate.

www.lisawoodruffnutrition.com/books

Hi! My name is Rebel and this is my brother Sam.

We love to eat pizza and ice cream.

We like to play at the park.

We like to read books

and watch baseball games.

This is our brother Luca. He is little but likes to play with us.

We read books together

and play at the park.

We also eat meals and snacks together.

Luca has food allergies. He is allergic to peanuts and eggs. This means he can get very sick if he eats a food with peanuts or eggs.

Many kids and adults have food allergies. Here are some foods that kids can be allergic to:

Peanut

Sesame

Eggs

Soy

Milk

WHEAT

&

Shellfish

FISH

Tree Nuts

SUNFLOWER SEEDS

Our friend Josh has an older sister with food allergies.
She is allergic to eggs, milk, tree nuts, kiwi, and garlic.

Our neighbor Destiny loves to dance. Her food allergies are wheat and milk.

Luca was just a baby when he had an allergic reaction to peanut butter. He was crying and had red bumps on his face.

Our mom and dad were upset and took him away from the table. We were very scared.

The next morning, our parents talked to us about food allergies. Now we know how to help keep our brother safe.

Luca sees a special type of doctor called an Allergist. His Allergist helped our family learn what foods he is allergic to and what foods are safe for him to eat.

Our mom and dad read food labels to make sure something is safe for Luca to eat.

We help by asking if food has peanuts or eggs. We also tell our family and friends that Luca has food allergies.

Our brother has medicine called an EpiPen. It is kept in a small bag that goes wherever Luca goes.

If he gets sick from his food allergy, then an adult will give him the EpiPen and call 911.

We help by reminding our parents or baby-sitters that Luca's EpiPen needs to come with us when we leave our house.

We can still eat food that Luca is allergic to, as long as we are careful to keep him safe.

Bread and noodles can be made with nuts or eggs. Candy and cookies can also have nuts or eggs.

Sometimes it's not safe to do things the way we used to before Luca got food allergies. We can't get ice cream with him because there are eggs and sometimes nuts. But we can get snow cones together!

Teal is the color of food allergy awareness. We are using colors to teach Luca about his food allergies.

Only Luca can use his teal plates, silverware, and cups. We bring his special dishes with us when we eat away from home.

We also keep our brother safe by washing our hands before and after we eat.

Finding new ways to do our favorite things can be hard.
But we love our brother and want to help keep him safe.

It is okay to have two feelings at the same time.

Is there someone in your family with food allergies? Food allergies can affect everyone in your family, **even you.**

You are loved and special too.

And now you have a very important job – to be a Food Allergy Helper!

How to be a Food Allergy Helper:

Be kind.

Wash hands before and after eating.

Ask questions and listen.

Don't share food without asking an adult.

Think of safe ways to play and celebrate.

CPSIA information can be obtained
at www.ICGtesting.com
Printed in the USA
LVHW072354130522
718744LV00007B/115